# Monversation
## A Journey to Healing

*A collection of random thoughts and*

*poetry*

**Dorina Owindi**

Monversation©

*Published in the Republic of Finland by:* Dorina Owindi/© Monversation Publishing

Cover Design and Illustration: Ellah Nyawira / Kukinta Design



First Printing, 2018

Second Printing, 2019

Printed by KDP

ISBN 978-952-69043-0-6 (paperback)

ISBN 978-952-69043-1-3 (hardback)

ISBN 978-952-69043-2-0 (E-Book)

ISBN 978-952-69043-3-7 (EPUB)

# Dedication

*This book is dedicated to the one's that tell themselves every day, that they have made it! The one's that live in doubt of their power. The one's that live in fear of becoming. The ones that have experienced loss, heartbreak, disappointment from the ones they love or have loved.*
*The silent everyday warriors who exist within us and amongst us.*

# Author's Note

My first vivid memory of writing a poem, I must have been about eleven or twelve years old. I remember I was angry at a friend whom, I felt had dismissed and disregarded my feelings. Then I struggled with anger management. The only way out was to-- write.

After I realised that it made me feel better, I kept at it. Expressing my innermost thoughts--till 2017, I have never dared share my poetry save for on an old blog where I used a pseudonym. My parents had no idea that I wrote poetry, and neither did my friends. Thus, this book is about coming out of my writing closet with my *monversations*.

Monversation, was born in 2016 and was based on quotes and conversations, I had with myself and clients. It depicts a conversation you have within your innermost thoughts that you hardly share with anyone.

I take you through my journey from 2002 till today These thoughts are a collection of my life through my naivety, crushes, infatuation, fighting depression, heartbreak and becoming. **When I Am Alone** is a collection of random thoughts and interlude if you may prefer, it isn't necessary poetry.

I hope this will inspire you to write, to feel, to heal and to thrive. That wherever you are in life that whatever you feel it shall pass. Let it live through you, learn to let it go, so it won't haunt you.

Loads of love,

Dorina Owindi

# **Monversation:** A Journey to Healing

# When I Was Lost

# Downward spiral

Was there a whisper in the wind or was it just a whistle?

I don't remember much or am I just a dreamer?

I don't know what to do, should I just keep it all in my chest?

Will I; have to spit it out or will I just have to let it rest?

I need someone, someone understanding,

Someone who will be there -- not resisting,

I need my peace of mind-- I need time,

I want freedom, freedom to be what I want to be,

I feel restrained in the world of me,

I'm lost, I can't find my way,

Will someone help me or will I have to stay,

Lost forever, frozen in time, while the world goes on, leaving
me behind,

Risk is something dangerous but, I must gamble,

It is give or take, there is no time to mumble,

I can't undo what has already been done,

But, I can't say that I am prepared to have none,

I've raced the race, I haven't won but I must, reach, my goal,

I know now it's time-- lights, camera action, to play my role,

# My Heart is Weak

I'm not inspired my heart is so weak, my strength is all gone
and my future so bleak,
Will, I see tomorrow?
I smile but its tight, hoping for a better response, but my heart
beat isn't right,
Why me?
I hate the way I am, I keep running but I keep hitting the wall
like a ram,
Why can't I change? I really want to turn the page,
Why can't I see the light? All I want to do is soar but, all I have;
is fright,
Am I going through a phase? What is it, with this human race?
I never got the answers though I have searched — why?
Now I am searching for a high, a high that will take me away
from this pain,
This pain of hating the person I see in the mirror, the person,
that I wish could see clearer,
Someone save me before I find myself lost so deep, when I look
at that window I desperately want to take that leap,
Staring at a very grey mirror my heart grows cold, I can't bring
myself to admit it, but maybe I should be so bold, leave with
my stories and worries untold.

Can anyone hear my silent screams? Or will I continue to be stuck in this nightmare they call a dream?

# Frustration

Can anybody answer my questions?

Without giving me pointless suggestions,

I am torn between, the past and the present

I can't leave it behind, it follows me like a shadow always

present,

I am unfocused and I vaguely remember the decent walks in

the park,

Why must my thoughts go towards the dark?

People glance my way and give me vague answers — so sly,

They don't understand me, nor do they try,

Yet they laugh and kill my remnants of hope,

I mess up and I'm tried like a criminal at large,

A fugitive who has to hide, hide from the truth — I can't purge,

I want to hide, I know I can't go back,

The place I once called home is a memory on a broken rack,

Tainted and tarnished like scrap metal sold,

The memories are mixed up, the rough edges bold,

Not many people can see, but texture has a way of being seen

even when not touched,

The dark memories often come in bits-- not rushed,

I look for a new door to open, I want it to surprise me with

something exciting, vibrant,

All I get is an eye sore, to escape-- I realise, in their eyes I must
be a vagrant,
Only time will tell, let my fate find a kinder destiny, As I hold
to my dignity that's so tiny,
The torture chamber banished and with it my pain vanished,
I shall stand as a new person, on my own two feet, write
chapters of my version.

# A Reflection of Darkness

A drunk you call me?

With your judgmental eyes filled with disapproval, as I sway,

you watch me,

I tend to stagger at my worst, crawl or puke, how I find my way

home is a fluke,

Some of you laugh at my actions, in your thoughts; the blame is

a cause of my negative attractions,

Did you ever consider this once, that the blame could be yours?

That my condition is a result of the circular tours,

I believe in living life to the fullest, but your intentions were

never the purest,

My action is a reaction, to the cause of seduction, that led me to

where I stand or rather struggling,

You call yourself a friend but, you hardly know or care about

the person to squabble,

You are intoxicated by your own selfishness, crying seems like a

waste thus, I indulge in your feigned sorry that is blemished,

Sure, I accept my situation but, not fully-- so I drown myself in

a liquid — I silently cry. Till this sickly-sweet situation makes me

bitter and dry.

Either way, the effect calms me in a way human company

cannot,

I am momentarily happy, so let me have this illusion-- though harshly,

Before you give me those disappointed looks, remember this moment for the books,

Ask yourselves if you truly are friends, detox from your selfishness and I won't have to make any amends,

I need to use my temporary crutch, sometimes I allow myself to have that forbidden touch,

Leave me now and let me phase out the world with my drunk fixation, see it in a version that makes sense in this intoxication.

# The Infatuation

You make me smile, even when I see you from a mile,
I can't get enough of you, I don't know whether I'm into you,
Maybe I'm infatuated by you, maybe I just like the way you,
the way you talk to me,
When you are wrong, I am intoxicated by your song,
I just don't see it as too bad, I guess you're the blinding factor I
never had,
Too bad I'm so far, but whenever we talk you sound so near,
I'm living in a world imagined in my head, I can't get you out
of my mind when I am thinking of you in my bed,
You make me feel so good, I am not sure whether I want you,
All I know is there IS some chemistry between us, I wonder
where the future will lead us,
I don't know whether you feel the same way, but if you don't
it's okay—hey,
For now, I am willing to settle for friends,
Though I know your past more than you know mine, all I know
is you are so fine!
Fine to be mine but, not now some other time.

# Unhealthy Encounter

I've resorted to step aside, as my feelings for you subside,

In the midst of intoxication, I hallucinate, thoughts of you I
can't help but illuminate,

I know deep down the closet space is new, it makes me smile
when I thought we'd make it to the pew,

In my thoughts a web of negativity, the magical sensation
unravelled into positivity,

I'd like to hold your hand, why is it when I try, you let go? I am
left deserted as if I was a throw,

Make me, understand all these feelings, as they are a result of
the hope you instilled, from the empty promises you said you
would fulfil,

All lost in the unconscious actions of you, that pierced, choked,
insomnisized this strong unfeeling,

It's a long time but you'll be mine one day, we will shine, and
bask in the rays of friendship, or pass each other on the
opposite side of those dangerous mines,

Or am I forever condemned, to your cold yet lukewarm trends?

My subconscious senses your presence, to think I'd thought of
resistance,

To think I hated and loathed the repercussions, yet loved and
embraced every moment, within, in my state of concussion,

# The Subscriber You Hurt Can't Be Reached

He comes like a thief in the night and strikes at an interval,

My presence to him is a state of continuous celebration like a
carnival,

He knows my vulnerability, but is eluded by the unsurety,

Studying my movements is a hobby, but he isn't just any thief,
he steals glances from the lobby,

He doesn't look for worldly possessions, he likes the chase and
leaving repercussions,

he wants your soul bare, to tear, he doesn't hesitate nor have no
fear,

Brutal and sneaky, lyrically armed, with the deep knowledge,
he toiled so hard to farm,

Impeccable manners, somehow, he manages to get everyone to
notice him like-- banners,

He needs someone with wit to undo him, although when he
walks in, there is a foreboding hymn,

He feels for his subject of interest but, price holds him back, he
falters takes his dues in a pack,

The very pride that pushed everyone else away, is the very
pride that leads him to stay at bay,

I take the bullshit not because I'm gullible, but out of obligation,

I see this scenario growing, becoming a play of volition,

I don't trust this con man, I recognise that now, beat him--- I

can,

The thief is a combination of my past and present, the reason

why there was a love descent,

Past should be what it is, he has to realize I never really was his,

Gnawing he is at my door, I am prepared and armed I am

crouching on the floor,

Con man doesn't know what is going to hit him, it won't be just

on his chin,

He keeps coming back, but doesn't get deeper, he is starting to

look like some kind of pervert—a peeper,

My surface won't peel, I froze all the layers where I feel,

Not for him, not for anyone anytime soon, I am cold and elusive

like the clouds in front of the shinning moon.

# The Lone Wolf

I thought I'd just let it go,

I just wanted to go with the flow,

But, now I don't think I can handle it,

I feel I'm wasting my time in the wild,

Maybe it is safer to go back to a crowd,

Can I really handle it that loud?

I don't know what I got myself into,

Though it's not too late to get out,

I just wanted to dance about,

I can't handle the competition,

I am losing my vision,

Don't know what I want to be,

All I know is this life is me,

Love it and hate it, can't change the past,

Want to find a light and make it last,

The rhythm's slow but picking up,

How long will it take before it reaches its climax?

Can anyone hear me?

# I Believe in I

I now believe I can conquer, I don't need to confer,

Once I make up my mind, I am not leaving my decision behind,

I'll take a chance when I see an open window, I'll take a chance
even if I won't win oh!

No one can be me,

I am unique within, I am strong though thin,

I am sweet, yet I can be mean, I am sane yet insane,

I am human yet classified as an animal, a species, a race, a
mammal,

Following my instinct, trying to discern and be distinct,

Hating what's ugly and trying to see potential, by investing
myself in it, it ends up getting detrimental,

Some things can be enhanced by others, some things you got to
leave them to chance,

Sometimes I get what I deserve, unrewarding gestures I tend to
reserve,

I don't give up easy, except on he's,

Especially, when I feel and see I don't deserve them or vice
versa,

I am capable, I now believe, I can retrieve

# When I Am Alone

# Silent Screams

But it's time for me to say no,

It's time to cut the chord,

I hate the scene and it really sucks,

The greatest thing is I have to quit and live the life I want to

lead,

Save me someone but, what if the whistle is telling me it must

be real,

Oh! come on! We had a deal, but I cannot let it go

See, for once, I just want to find me,

Not the runner, from morning to night,

Not the girl, who is frightened by light,

Want you to help me escape, I am tired of waiting

Tired of seeing myself being plucked slowly into an apetalous

bud,

I have got to find myself before it's too late,

It's time I stopped the self-hate,

Hate that could destroy my world in a thud!

# I am tired

My flow is so slow, my heart is hollow unfeeling, yet empty, though still unfeeling.

Nothing brings my sense of emotion, I lost with it my desire of devotion,

I yoyo and its official, I can't tell the difference between what's real and the superficial,

Why now? Why today? Why not now?

I am who I am and yet, I hide from me

# SOS

In need of uplifting,

My mind is floating, though lost in stagnation

The reason impenetrable yet bare, finding an answer is a trip I

swear,

Truly! insanity paved the way, I am not in a hurry to arrive at

the latter.

# When You Ghosted Me

Because I miss you and I can't stop thinking about you,

Because I miss you, our moments together bring my smile alive,

Hope you know I really miss you and that's all!

Its great the connection we had, everything about you doesn't

make me sad

Except, I can't be with you I can't feel you, my heart will always

be with you as much as I tried to forget and deny,

My suitcase of memories flash in my eyes, if you were an

accessory you'd be my sentimental necklace,

If you were stolen, I'd find a replacement, even though it would

never be the same

# Reluctantly letting you slip

My happiness, my sadness

I'll wallow in my freedom though, a piece of you I can't let go,

too tough!

# When the tears keep flooding

As the floods try to break through the gates, their pressure
breaks down the steady walls in stat,
The flood breaks down the gates, solidity is what the mind
states,
Hollowness grows within,
Lost in the torrent of water, the bubbles subside and falter,
The stones of debris sink, the rays of the sun blink
The stillness, a sign of a storm beginning

# The Replay of lies

When you told me that you loved me, did you think I'd believe
your lie?

When you told me that you missed me, did you think I'd cry?

You see you've hurt me too many times, hell I made it easy the
second time,

Now I'm dead and have no feelings, you crushed them I've had
it to the ceiling,

I asked myself, many times, why I do this? Why am I so foolish?

# The Constant Labelling that Diminishes Pieces of Me

They say your booty is African, your mentality is European,

They say you've been spoilt, your personality they avoid,

If you'd worried about that dive, you wouldn't be here

spreading your fever,

Your energy is unmatched, your possibilities unhatched,

Opportunities treading, working on that spelling,

Leave your mark, because it isn't easy being you! It's work!

# Awe, fear and reverence

Drama mama on the scene, such a lady never obscene,

Oops! We all make mistakes we aren't perfect,

But people can't help but think you're perfect,

Kind of hard been looked up to; by people who you hardly

even imagined would,

Life's a mystery, a sequence of unsolved mysteries,

They say they know you, but you know who you are,

Incredible, indigenous, exotic mama, you've got it, people wish

they had it,

That's why they put you down, your silence and aloofness hurt

them,

They want you to break!

Girl, you are going, to have that cake!

# Almost Acceptance

I've reached a point of truce, an internal external battle,

They can't stop running their mouths,

They can't stop checking me out,

Judging is all they do, Jealousy is what their soul's brew

I'm the palm tree amongst the acacia's

I am indigenous exotic, you heard right indigenous exotic

I keep it real, I am not afraid to know the deal,

No use beating about the bush, I may be gone before you admit

the truth

# Who is Fooling Whom?

Being human is to be constantly bombarded with complexities. The struggle with being aware of self, then others projecting their insecurities on you. You never can be just right, just perfect. You either speak the wrong language or wear the wrong colour. If those are right, then you do not belong because of your materialistic value, your physical appearance or appeal. It's a constant battle to define something indefinable outside. When the lights are turned off and we are alone and stuck with demons we distract ourselves and constantly wish away that white elephant...

Life is complex but why do we make it so hard on our being & spirit? When did acceptance, become such a chore?

When did acceptance become something that makes people feel uncomfortable?... When did…? It doesn't matter...What I can do today, is be in my own personal school & educate myself on who I really am. Without my roles & earthly titles. Without my squad that validates me.

I am whole, broken but I let the light shine through because even if they don't accept my appearance. My presence already shook something in them. That. Is. Power...

# Metamorphosis

We are truly infinite, when we realize our power. That whatever we choose to create, may indeed live on, beyond our century, era or generation. That everything that happens is just, history repeating itself. The only difference is the source of information that is readily available to us, if we lose the distractions. Surely, if people can build buildings, bridges and ships? They said metal is too heavy to fly and can sink. Then why do we have planes or cruise ships? Why do we limit ourselves to the caterpillar that refuses to become a butterfly? When will we acknowledge that metamorphosis only happens, when we work on changing ourselves?

# When I Got the Nudge

# Burning Bridges

I've been burned so many times often filled with rage,

So, disappointed, hurt but I've learnt to let go and turn the page,

I give my all or so it seems, it feels like a glass that's filled with liquid but still wants more,

Dripping on the sides when it can't take anymore,

Sadly, this IS life and they're here, No I will not break, I won't shed a tear,

As much as I cherish the time spent, there is no going back to where I went,

It is all over, roll over, they are just a memory,

I am done being your doormat, wiped, abused and stepped on so you can raise your hat,

It may seem easy to cross me, but crossing back that burnt bridge is beyond me,

You ignited the fire and did what you did, you waited in the corner watched and hid,

I hate that I gave you a place in my heart, so you could stab it and try to rip it apart,

Thank you for showing me who you truly are, I will be rooting and admiring your success from afar,

The door was open but, now its shut this friendship has ended
and that is that!

# Letters to Self-Love

When love doesn't seem enough, the way we treat ourselves so rough,

Why do I have to look for validation, why do I sabotage myself through condemnation,

I want to stay healthy but, I eat the very thing that's unhealthy

I want to be honest but, I keep telling myself lies — dishonesty,

My clothes don't fit, I blame the person who made them for changing the sizes,

I wallow in self-pity for way too long, by the time I snap out of it, my time has gone

The window of opportunity, to make my journey easier-- is gone,

I had a mole hill and now it's an Everest,

Why do I do this to myself?

Why can't I love myself enough to care about my well-being,

Instead, I live life as a fraction of a being,

Excuses when confronted, attacking people that were only trying to help,

People say let sleeping dogs lie,

Is that what I have become?

Someone so difficult to live with?

When love doesn't seem enough, I sabotage myself and blame
everyone else for my demise,
Red flags, Sirens, my heart constantly sinking but, I didn't heed
the warnings,
They were for someone else, How, did I get here?
I drown myself in things that do not nourish or help my soul,
They numb the pain for a moment, just a moment
What have I done to myself?
When self-love is not enough!

# When I had to Let Go

# A Letter to the one that got away

The love I have for you runs deep, sometimes I ran away just to come back for a peep,

I used to hope and pray you were okay, sometimes it would pain my heart that to you, I was just a play,

I care for you without event thinking, but the more I thought of you my heart kept sinking,

For my own sanity, I had to let you go, because being without you made me feel so low,

Those feelings are buried deep, these ones won't come for a peep

I accepted you don't love me back, so now I live my life constantly hoping to pack,

The feelings are dead not dormant, I have healed from constantly being your doormat,

# When I discovered the Monster in You

I can't breathe. I can't think.

Every step I take makes me falter, as I hear the echo of the cold-hearted words you uttered,

The tears keep wallowing in my eyes I can't let you know, now, that you are not in my presence, I let it flow,

I was hit by a silencer, one shot to my heart, the other to all the memories, that connected us-- are lost in a chart,

Everything I thought I knew about us, every ounce of respect I thought you had, you let pass,

I suck in air and let out a sound high pitched and heavy with emotion, but there's an emotion-- I haven't been able to identify since you peeled your layers in quick motion,

Is this anguish mixed with an air of betrayal?

Anguish, because I am angry,

I got myself into this mess, why am I surprised? You have constantly been my source of stress.

Betrayal because you claimed I was your best friend?! With the way things are going, there will be no room to attempt to amend,

Or betrayal because your lack of honouring your word reared its ugly head again?

I am shaking. I am wet. I am cold.

This walking in the rain and crying out loud to hide my pain in a foreign street,

It is the only way I could get away from you, so I would not use my fists, to beat,

No one would blame me, as I was justified especially, if I had to testify,

About the mental beating you put me through, you did it with a smile, a smirk in your own twisted mind-- you tried to push me through,

Punishment, because all I did was love you, I noticed you were self-destructing,

I stupidly tried to help and that help became a special kind of hell,

A hell, where I allowed you to steal my joy, which you happily showed off like a brand-new toy,

While I was drowning, and struggling to find my smile, my happiness,

All you did was deliberately try to contribute to my sadness,

The power you had over me was so surreal,

I froze, I hesitated, all I could think of —"When will I stop being that hamster on a wheel?"

I shudder to think, that it was you, who would make me lose faith in-- you, love and people,

I hope that one day, you will know and feel the magnitude of the mess you created and remember that boomerang called karma is not unrelated.

# A Letter to Freedom

My heart got pierced again by you, I told myself time and time
again I could live without you,

I chose to focus on your kindness, your good deeds and the lace
of lies contributed to my blindness,

All you are, is like everybody else,

Tit for tat is the language you speak, you don't understand that
your kindness came in streaks,

Your kindness was based on how much you blew that puff of
smoke, without it you were the fire without smoke,

I used to feel sorry for you,

After you pierced my heart again, made me wail and weep for
the time I lost,

The time I was afraid to walk away, I loved you too much to be
a ghost,

The time you made me feel guilty for considering cutting the
chord,

The time when you reminded me, how I couldn't find someone
like you,

The times you implored on me that you couldn't live without
me,

Sometimes I sit down and think, how could this be?

I gave my body, my mind, my soul,

My time, my money, my whole,

All I got was a reminder of past mistakes,

You liked it better when I was your steak,

You could decide my fate,

How you manipulated me claiming things on a silver platter,

How can you justify that you love me, when all you do is hurt me?

I cried countless of times, my tears were heavy and were bitter as the limes,

Why won't you set me free?

Why do you want to just be?

Why are you trying to manipulate me?

The more you play those games, the more I am glad I never had to change my names,

I never had to promise to be with you forever,

When I used to love you,

You were an integral part but, now I know you as the guy who pierced my heart.

# When I awakened

45

# An Apology Letter

I am sorry for not honouring you when you screamed you couldn't handle it,

I gagged your screams, I let you be around people who did more harm than good,

Who misused your time, who strengthened your insecurities and fears,

Let you diminish your love for yourself, I am sorry that I never allowed you to grow,

That I would let you brush away the things you already know,

Just to have yourself with palm in hand, wishing that people didn't think you would always be part of their band,

Synchronized yet not in sync, very often you'd do things that made your heart sink,

I am sorry that you haven't learned to forgive yourself, I am thankful that you're slowly learning a lesson,

I am thankful you're learning to embrace your being,

I promise I will love you more, protect you and listen to you,

Till death do us part, I will love you eternally,

Signed your dead ego on behalf of your mind and soul.

# You Open My Heart

It's crazy how I never noticed you, or did I?

Your smile lights up the room, you know how to sweep away worries with your broom,

Your actions always speak louder than your words, you make me laugh hours on end, you are a healer,

When you speak passionately about what you stand for, you are a feeler,

I am blessed to have you in my life, even though I do not understand what's going on inside,

Why have I never noticed you? Why have I never seen you?

Or did I ignore it, because I knew, you and I couldn't be true,

I am definitely confused about, the way I feel for you,

In one way, you are family, we look out for each other,

On the other hand, our friendship runs deep,

We've seen each other through tough times,

We are still here, I don't know what's going to happen next,

But I know there is something in you, I want to have in this life,

Maybe more in my love life.

You're a blueprint.

I shouldn't settle and I thank you for that lesson.

# A letter to Love

I love-love, that's what I want, someone who loves me deeply,

compliments me-- that I am proud of, that I make proud,

someone whose soul sings,

understands my — our world without pings,

Able to stay present and relish in the beauty of our world.

Understands and tries to heal the pain in their world,

Compassion exudes in their heart, you don't have to explain

what's ethical, they just know.

Someone who understands, I am a mystical queen

I have gone through many battles and wars to claim my throne.

Someone who understands my body, someone who

understands movement,

Someone who respects my soul and honours it, is not put off by

it

Someone who understands my struggles in the physical but,

doesn't dismiss it

Someone who knows about growth, ambition and works smart,

Honest, kind and nothing to hide,

Full of love but understands the pain inside.

Someone willing to be galactic, someone ready to step into their

power.

# A Letter to Healing

I know you are here but, it is hard to let go,

Even more difficult is when I see you in my dreams,

One moment we are having a conversation, we are all together,

mingling and conversing,

In the morning, the reality of it all hits me. You are in a space

where there is no concept of time,

I can reach you but, at the same time I do not want to, because it

makes everything real,

Good thing is, there are no remnants of hate, anger or

resentment towards you,

If anything, your actions taught me, you were human too.

Flawed.


Sometimes, I would feel ashamed, other times-- it didn't matter.

At least the pain I feel from watching you deteriorate are gone. I

sometimes think of your jokes and how funny you were,

I just need to shake off the exhaustion, I feel like my, hear plugs

are blocked.

I am heart broken. The reality is I gave my heart and soul, the

romantic love died with you.

If this is the pain I feel and you were just dad. Then how does

mum feel 40 years?!

Would I be equipped to handle that pain again?

Loss has been the theme of 2016 but, I know things will change.

Please do not visit my dreams unless you have a message.

Waking up, to know you are there but, are not-- is painful.

I love you and I miss you. Give me time please. I want to heal.

The wounds are still too raw but, I cover them well.

# Where I Am

Home...

Home used to be where you were,

Where you and I, laid our heads together,

A safe haven, especially, when the world around me seemed

tough,

I would run home because, somehow being with you, the world

didn't seem so rough,

Your arms, I would look forward to being wrapped in your

embrace,

I realized that somehow you were my saving grace,

Home...

A place I longed for, craved for, wanted more than anything,

Then that fateful day happened when you broke my trust,

When you took me in a way I hadn't agreed to, with your

thrust,

You were pleased with yourself, I couldn't live with myself

Then you left and that was the beginning of the end,

I noticed your disregard, nonchalance and indifference.

I had placed you, over my own happiness and desires,

I just wanted a home.

Then I realized, home is me... home is where I am, how I feel,

how I love, how I greet the day,

It's not really a place, it's a mindset,

It's the one place where my bed is but, it's also the place I nurture,

Home should not make you angry, sad, negative and disconnected...

Home is where you come to recharge,

when the world tells you to stay connected,

You can switch off and stay disconnected

Even though you are not there,

Now, I have; learnt that

# About the Author

Photo by Jarno Valtonen

Dorina Owindi's writing style has been described as deep, intense, intuitive, expressive and thought provoking. Reading her texts evokes introspection; allowing readers to hold space, be and reconnect to the subconscious mind. Her debut book Monversation: A journey to healing was first published in 2018 as an ebook. Her belief that writing can be a healing process has been backed by science studies thus she uses her educational background and passion to coach people into *healing writing*. Dorina spends her time between Europe and Africa. Currently working on releasing the follow up book Monversation volume

2 by the Summer of 2019.

# Acknowledgement

Thank you for purchasing this book and going through this journey with me. I have selected a few of these, to create an audio album. It's intended for those who are visually impaired and those that do not have the patience to read.

I would like to thank first and foremost the Universe, for allowing me to have different experiences that have pushed me "out of the closet" so to speak. If I did not go through my up and downs, mess ups and was perfect, I would have nothing to contribute to the world.

My guides for pushing me to complete my projects and not falling into procrastination. Waking me up and helping me discover hidden gems, I had forgotten about. Reminding me how far, I had come especially, when I felt inadequate.

Thank you to Alexis Jones for helping me plant seeds, so that I can create the life I want. Live in my truth and most importantly not be afraid to speak and share my truth. Who knew, an encounter in 2013, would blossom to a loving and supportive friendship that has brought the following people in my life:

Thank you to my beautiful fellow soulpreneurs, my coaches Tiffany Lanier and Lorraine Whyte. For helping me gain clarity and showing me how it is done through leading by example. I would like to thank Marci Onsinyo and Carol Mae Whittick for listening to the audio and encouraging me to put my work out there. Being a constant source of support, clarity and cheering me on, during this creative journey.

Finally, I would like to thank the people who constantly support my work and keep putting the word out there. Inspire me by the way they contribute to the world by following their dreams. Elias Kahla, Duncan Ndirangu, Christine Mwiti, Christine Langinauer, Ellah Nyawira and Elina Ojanen. Last but not least my dearest mama and my honorary aunt Ms. Thompson for constantly supporting me and keeping me in your prayers.